Bob & Myrna.

To Dear P...

Our Love,
The Rouse's.

Leaves of
Comfort

Leaves of Comfort

Words of Hope and Solace
for Troubled Times

GREENWICH HOUSE
NEW YORK

This 1982 edition is published by Greenwich House, a division of
Arlington House, Inc., distributed by
Crown Publishers, Inc.

Manufactured in the United States of America

Library of Congress Cataloging in Publication Data
Main entry under title:

Leaves of comfort.

1. Anthologies.
PN6014.L423   1982   808.8   82-15485
ISBN: 0-517-386313 (jacketed edition)
ISBN: 0-517-386321 (suede edition)

h g f e d c b a

FOREWORD

"The lowest ebb is the turn of the tide."
Henry Wadsworth Longfellow

Leaves of Comfort is a collection of quotations for the difficult times in our lives—times of loss, serious illness, pain or grief. At these moments we feel alone and vulnerable, in need of comfort and support.

Leaves of Comfort offers the wisdom of well-known writers—Robert Louis Stevenson, Mark Twain, Henry Wadsworth Longfellow, Victor Hugo, George Eliot, William Shakespeare, Rudyard Kipling and others—to strengthen us and give us a feeling of universal fellowship.

Although the words in *Leaves of Comfort* cannot erase all our pain and grief, we can find solace and a lessening of sorrow by sharing the thoughts and feelings of others who have been in similar situations.

Pain and loss are part of the human experience, but they do not have to destroy us. They can help us to a fuller appreciation of life, to the realization that our darkest moments will pass and that what we thought was our lowest ebb actually is the turn of the tide.

ELEGY WRITTEN IN A COUNTRY CHURCHYARD

The curfew tolls the knell of parting day,
　The lowing herds wind slowly o'er the lea,
The ploughman homeward plods his weary way,
　And leaves the world to darkness and to me.

Now fades the glimmering landscape on the sight,
　And all the air a solemn stillness holds,
Save where the beetle wheels his droning flight,
　And drowsy tinklings lull the distant folds:

Save that from yonder ivy-mantled tower,
　The moping owl does to the moon complain
Of such as, wand'ring near her secret bower,
　Molest her ancient, solitary reign.

Beneath those rugged elms, that yew-trees' shade,
　Where heaves the turf in many a mold'ring heap,
Each in his narrow cell forever laid,
　The rude forefathers of the hamlet sleep.

The breezy call of incense-breathing morn,
　The swallow twitt'ring from the straw-built shed,
The cock's shrill clarion, of the echoing morn,
　No more shall rouse them from their lowly bed.

For them no more the blazing hearth shall burn,
　Or busy housewife ply her evening care;
No children run to lisp their sire's return,
　Or climb his knees the envied kiss to share.

1

Oft did the harvest to their sickle yield,
　　Their furrow oft the stubborn glebe has broke;
How jocund did they drive their team afield!
　　How bowed the woods beneath their sturdy stroke!

Let not ambition mock their useful toil,
　　Their homely joys, and destiny obscure;
Nor grandeur hear with a disdainful smile
　　The short and simple annals of the poor.

The boast of heraldry, the pomp of pow'r,
　　And all that beauty, all that wealth e'er gave,
Await alike th' inevitable hour.
　　The paths of glory head but to the grave.

Nor you, ye proud, impute to these the fault,
　　If memory o'er their tomb no trophies raise,
Where thro' the long-drawn aisle and fretted vault,
　　The pealing anthem swells the note of praise.

Can storied urn, or animated bust,
Back to its mansion call the fleeting breath?
Can honor's voice provoke the silent dust,
　　Or flatt'ry soothe the dull cold ear of Death?

Perhaps in this neglected spot is laid
　　Some heart once pregnant with celestial fire;
Hands that the rod of empire might have sway'd,
　　Or waked to ecstasy the living lyre.

But knowledge to their eyes her ample page,
   Rich with the spoils of time, did ne'er unroll;
Chill penury repressed their noble rage,
   And froze the genial current of the soul.

Full many a gem of purest ray serene
   The dark unfathomed caves of ocean bear;
Full many a flower is born to blush unseen,
   And waste its sweetness on the desert air.

Thomas Gray

IF WE HAD THE TIME

If I had the time to find a place
And sit me down full face to face
With my better self that stands no show
In my daily life that rushes so,
It might be then I would see my soul
Was stumbling still toward the shining goal—
I might be nerved by the thought sublime,
       If I had the time!

If I had the time to let my heart
Speak out and take in my life a part,
To look about and stretch a hand
To a comrade quartered on no-luck land,
Ah, God! If I might but just sit still
And hear the note of the whip-poor-will,
I think that my wish with God would rhyme—
       If I had the time!

If I had the time to learn from you
How much for comfort my word would do;
And I told you then of my sudden will
To kiss your feet when I did you ill—
If the tears aback of the bravado
Could force their way and let you know—
Brothers, the souls of us all would chime,
       If we had the time!

THE LORD IS MY SHEPHERD!

1 The Lord is my shepherd; I shall not want.

2 He maketh me to lie down in green pastures; he leadeth me beside the still waters.

3 He restoreth my soul; he leadeth me in the paths of righteousness for his name's sake.

4 Yea, though I walk through the valley of the shadow of death, I will fear no evil; for thou art with me; thy rod and they staff they comfort me.

5 Thou preparest a table before me in the presence of mine enemies; thou anointest my head with oil; my cup runneth over.

6 Surely goodness and mercy shall follow me all the days of my life; and I will dwell in the house of the Lord forever.

Psalms XXIII

NOW I LAY ME DOWN TO SLEEP

Now I lay me down to sleep,
I pray Thee, Lord, my soul to keep.
If I should die before I wake
I pray Thee, Lord, my soul to take
And this I ask for Jesus' sake.
Amen.

HORACE GREELEY'S SORROW

My Friend:—The loss of my boy makes a great change in my feelings, plans and prospects. The joy of my life was comprehended in his, and I do not now feel that any personal object can strongly move me henceforth. I had thought of buying a country place, but it was for him. I had begun to love flowers and beautiful objects, because he liked them. Now, all that deeply concerns me is the evidence that we shall live hereafter, and especially that we shall live with and know those we loved here. I mean to act my part while life is spared me, but I no longer covet length of days. If I felt sure on the point of identifying and being with our loved ones in the world to come, I would prefer not to live long. As it is, I am resigned to whatever may be divinely ordered. . . . We had but few hours to prepare for our loss. He went to bed as hearty and happy as ever. At 5 A. M. he died. . . . His mother had bought him a fiddle the day before, which delighted him beyond measure; and he was only induced to lay it up at night by his delight at the idea of coming up in the morning and surprising me by playing on it before I got up. In the morning at daylight I was called to his bedside. The next day, I followed him to his grave! You cannot guess how golden and lovely his long hair (never cut) looked in the coffin. . . . Pickie was five years old last March. So much grace and wit and poetry were rarely or never blended in so young a child,

6

and to us his form and features were the perfection of beauty. We can never have another child, and life cannot be long enough to efface, though it will temper this sorrow. It differs in kind as well as degree from all that we have hitherto experienced.

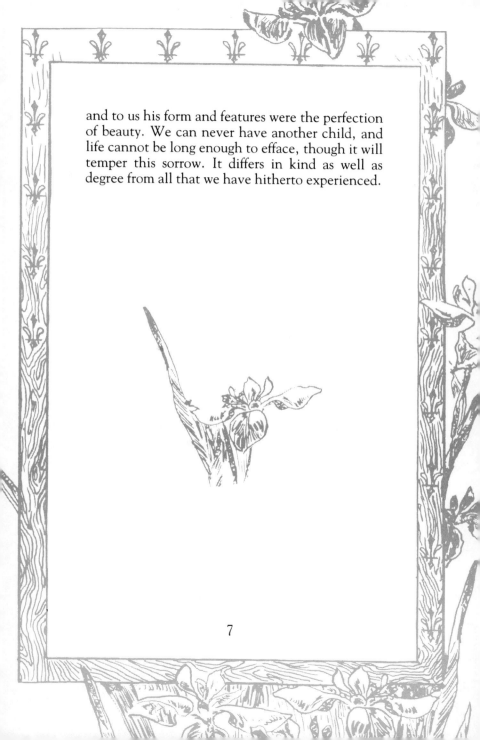

GOD MOVES IN A MYSTERIOUS WAY

God moves in a mysterious way
    His wonders to perform;
He plants his footsteps in the sea,
    And rides upon the storm.

Deep in unfathomable mines,
    With never-failing skill,
He treasures up his bright designs,
    And works his sovereign will.

Judge not the Lord by feeble sense,
    But trust him for his grace;
Behind a frowning providence
    He hides a smiling face.

His purposes will ripen fast,
    Unfolding every hour;
The bud may have a bitter taste,
    But sweet will be the flower.

Blind unbelief is sure to err,
    And scan his work in vain;
God is his own interpreter,
    And he will make it plain.

Ye fearful saints fresh courage take,
The clouds you so much dread
Are big with mercy and shall break,
With blessings on your head.

William Cowper

A JUNE MORNING

Oh! have you not seen on some morning in June,
When the flowers were in tears and the forest in
tune,
When the billows of morn broke bright on the air,
On the breast of the brightest, some star clinging
there?
Some sentinel star not ready to set,
Forgetting to wane and watching there yet?

How you gazed on that vision of beauty the while,
How it wavered till torn by the light of God's smile,
How it passed through the portals of pearl like a
bride,
How it paled as it passed and the morning star
died.
The sky was all blushes; the lark was all bliss,
And the prayer of your heart was "Be my ending
like this."

So my beautiful dove passed away from life's even;
So the blush of her being was blended with heaven;
So the bird of my bosom fluttered up in the dawn,
A window was open; my darling was gone.
A truant from tears, from time and from sin,
For the angel on watch took the wanderer in.

And when I shall hear the new song that she sings
I shall know her again, notwithstanding her wings,
By those eyes full of heaven; by the light of her
   hair,
And the smile she wore here she will surely wear
   there.

THE DAY IS DONE

The day is done, and the darkness
    Falls from the wings of Night,
As a feather is wafted downward
    From an eagle in his flight.

I see the lights of the village
    Gleam through the rain and the mist,
And a feeling of sadness comes o'er me
    That my soul cannot resist:

A feeling of sadness and longing,
    That is not akin to pain,
And resembles sorrow only
    As the mist resembles the rain.

Come, read to me some poem,
    Some simple and heartfelt lay,
That shall soothe this restless feeling,
    And banish the thoughts of day.

Not from the grand old masters,
    Not from the bards sublime,
Whose distant footsteps echo
    Through the corridors of Time.

For like strains of martial music,
    Their mighty thoughts suggest
Life's endless toil and endeavor;
    And tonight I long for rest.

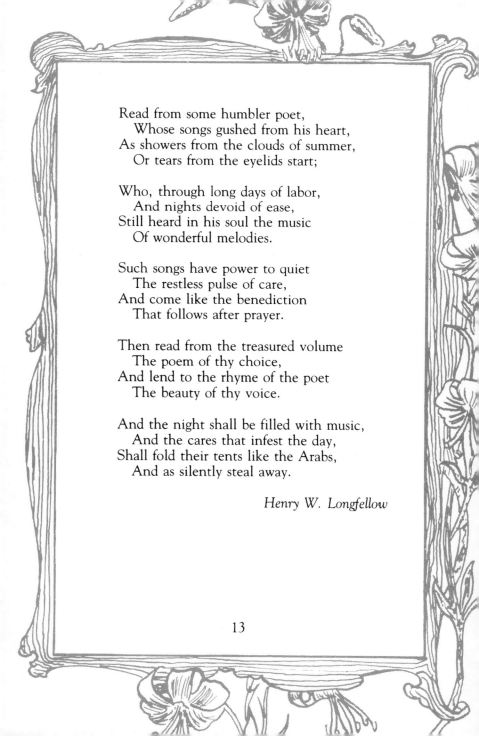

Read from some humbler poet,
  Whose songs gushed from his heart,
As showers from the clouds of summer,
  Or tears from the eyelids start;

Who, through long days of labor,
  And nights devoid of ease,
Still heard in his soul the music
  Of wonderful melodies.

Such songs have power to quiet
  The restless pulse of care,
And come like the benediction
  That follows after prayer.

Then read from the treasured volume
  The poem of thy choice,
And lend to the rhyme of the poet
  The beauty of thy voice.

And the night shall be filled with music,
  And the cares that infest the day,
Shall fold their tents like the Arabs,
  And as silently steal away.

Henry W. Longfellow

13

RESIGNATION

There is no flock, however watched and tended,
  But one dead lamb is there!
There is no fireside, howsoe'er defended,
  But has one vacant chair!

The air is full of farewells to the dying,
  And mournings for the dead;
The heart of Rachel, for her children crying,
  Will not be comforted!

Let us be patient! These severe afflictions
  Not from the ground arise,
But oftentimes celestial benedictions
  Assume this dark disguise.

We see but dimly through the mists and vapors;
  Amid these earthly damps,
What seem to us but sad funereal tapers
  May be heaven's distant lamps.

There is no Death! What seems so is transition.
  This life of mortal breath
Is but a suburb of the life elysian,
  Whose portal we call Death.

She is not dead—the child of our affection—
  But gone unto that school
Where she no longer needs our poor protection,
  And Christ himself doth rule.

In that great cloister's stillness and seclusion,
  By guardian angels led,
Safe from temptation, safe from sin's pollution,
  She lives, whom we call dead.

Day after day we think what she is doing
  In those bright realms of air;
Year after year, her tender steps pursuing,
  Behold her grown more fair.

Thus do we walk with her, and keep unbroken
  The bond which nature gives,
Thinking that our remembrance, though unspoken,
  May reach her where she lives.

Not as a child shall we again behold her
  For when with raptures wild
In our embraces we again enfold her,
  She will not be a child;

But a fair maiden, in her Father's mansion,
  Clothed with celestial grace;
And beautiful with all the soul's expansion
  Shall we behold her face.

And though at times impetuous with emotion
  And anguish long suppressed,
The swelling heart heaves moaning like the ocean,
  That cannot be at rest.

We will be patient, and assuage the feeling
  We may not wholly stay;
By silence sanctifying, not concealing,
  The grief that must have way.

Henry W. Longfellow

THE SIMPLE FAITH

Before me, even as behind,
God is, and all is well.

John Greenleaf Whittier

GOD IS AWAKE

Have courage for the great sorrows of life and
patience for the small ones. And when you have
finished your daily task, go to sleep in peace. God
is awake.

Victor Hugo

THE MOST PRECIOUS REWARD

Praise is well, compliment is well, but affection—
that is the last and *final* and most precious reward
that any man can win, whether by character or
achievement.

Mark Twain

17

THE DAYS GONE BY

Oh, the days gone by! Oh, the days gone by!
The apples in the orchard, and the pathway through
the rye;
The chirrup of the robin, and the whistle of the
quail
As he piped across the meadows sweet as any
night ingale;
When the bloom was on the clover and the blue
was in the sky,
And my happy heart brimmed over in the days
gone by.

In the days gone by, when my naked feet were
tripped
By the honeysuckle tangles where the water lilies
dripped,
And the ripples of the river lipped the moss along
the brink
Where the placid-eyed and lazy-footed cattle came
to drink,
And the tilting snipe stood fearless of the truant's
wayward cry
And the splashing of the swimmer, in the days
gone by.

Oh, the days gone by! Oh, the days gone by!
The music of the laughing lip, the luster of the
eye;
The childish faith in fairies, and Aladdin's magic
ring—

18

The simple, soul-reposing glad belief in everything—
When life was like a story, holding neither sob nor
  sigh,
In the golden olden glory of the days gone by.

James Whitcomb Riley

ROCK OF AGES—THE HYMN

Rock of Ages, cleft for me,
Let me hide myself in Thee.
Let the water and the blood
From thy riven side which flowed,
Be of sin the double cure.
Save from guilt and make me pure.

Could my tears forever flow;
Could my seal no languor know;
These for sin could not atone,
Thou must save, and Thou alone.
Rock of Ages cleft for me,
Let me hide myself in thee.

Not the labor of my hands
Can fulfill Thy law's demands;
Could my seal no respite know,
Could my tears forever flow,
All for sin could not atone;
Thou must save and Thou alone.

Nothing in my hand I bring;
Simply to Thy cross I cling.
Naked, come to Thee for dress,
Helpless, look to Thee for grace.
Foul, I to the Fountain fly,
Wash me, Savior, or I die.

While I draw this fleeting breath,
When mine eyes shall close in death.
When I rise to worlds unknown,
See Thee on Thy judgment throne—
Rock of Ages, cleft for me,
Let me hide myself in Thee.

AWAY

I cannot say, and I will not say
That he is dead. He is just away!

With a cheery smile and a wave of the hand,
He has wandered into an unknown land,

And left us dreaming how very fair
It needs must be, since he lingers there.

And you—oh, you, who the wildest yearn
for the old-time step and the glad return—

Think of him faring on, as dear
In the love of There as the love of Here;

And loyal still, as he gave the blows
Of his warrior stength to his country's foes—

Mild and gentle, as he was brave,
When the sweetest love of his life he gave

To simple things; where the violets grew
Pure as the eyes they were likened to,

The touches of his hands have strayed
As reverently as his lips have prayed;

When the little brown thrush that harshly chirred
Was dear to him as the mocking-bird;

And he pitied as much as a man in pain
A writhing honey-bee wet with rain.

Think of him still as the same, I say;
He is not dead—he is just—away!

James Whitcomb Riley

FOUND BY THE SHEPHERD

The sun from on high his glory flinging
    Filled all the land with a golden glow;
And the glad light fell o'er a mother singing
    A tender lullaby, sweet and low:
"My lamb! my lamb! may the Shepherd behold
    thee
    As He did the little ones of yore,
And safe in His loving arms enfold thee
    For evermore! Oh, for evermore!"

Ah me! ah me! o'er the brightest morning
    The storm may break and the storm-clouds fly;
And the fairest flowers life's path adorning
    Spring up and blossom but to die.
The sunlight fades and the shadows thicken,
    A chill wind blows from a far-off shore,
And the mother's arms, to her heart sore stricken,
    Shall clasp her darling—ah! nevermore.

But as the bright arch through the storm comes
    shining
    And tells of the mercy that cannot cease,
So now, through the storm of her sad repining,
    There comes a glad whisper of hope and peace:
"Thy lamb that was lost, lo! the Shepherd found it
    And safe to His own green pastures bore;
And the everlasting arms are around it
    For evermore! Oh, for evermore!"

24

I SHALL NOT PASS AGAIN THIS WAY

The bread that bringeth strength I want to give,
The water pure that bids the thirsty live:
I want to help the fainting day by day;
I'm sure I shall not pass again this way.

I want to give the oil of joy for tears,
The faith to conquer crowding doubts and fears.
Beauty for ashes may I give always:
I'm sure I shall not pass again this way.

I want to give good measure running o'er,
And into angry hearts I want to pour
The answer soft that turneth wrath away;
I'm sure I shall not pass again this way.

I want to give to others hope and faith,
I want to do all that the Master saith;
I want to live aright from day to day;
I'm sure I shall not pass again this way.

THE LOWEST EBB

The lowest ebb is the turn of the tide.

Henry Wadsworth Longfellow

THE GOLDEN SIDE

There is many a rest in the road of life.
   If we only would stop to take it,
And many a tone from the better hand,
   If the querulous heart would wake it!
To the sunny soul that is full of hope,
   And whose beautiful trust ne'er faileth,
The grass is green and the flowers are bright,
   Though the wintry storm prevaileth.

Better to hope, though, the clouds hang low,
   And to keep the eyes still lifted;
For the sweet blue sky will soon peep through,
   When the ominous clouds are rifted!
There was never a night without a day,
   Or an evening without a morning,
And the darkest hour, as the proverb goes,
   Is the hour before the dawning.

There is many a gem in the path of life
   Which we pass in our idle pleasure,
That is richer far than the jewelled crown
   Or the miser's hoarded treasure;
It may be the love of a little child,
   Or a mother's prayer to Heaven;
Or only a beggar's grateful thanks
   For a cup of water given.

Better to weave in the web of life
  A bright and golden filling,
And to do God's will with a ready heart
  And hands that are swift and willing,
Than to snap the delicate, slender threads
  Of our curious lives asunder,
And then blame Heaven for the tangled ends,
  And sit and grieve and wonder.

HAIL, SOVEREIGN LOVE

Hail, sovereign love, which first began
The scheme to rescue fallen man!
Hail, matchless, free, eternal grace,
Which gave my soul a Hiding Place.

Against the God who built the sky,
I fought with hands uplifted high,
Despised the mention of His grace,
Too proud to seek a Hiding Place.

Enwrapt in thick Egyptian night,
And fond of darkness more than light,
Madly I ran the sinful race,
Secure, without a Hiding Place.

And thus the eternal counsel ran,
Almighty love, arrest that man!
I felt the arrows of distress,
And found I had no Hiding Place.

Indignant justice stood aview
To Sinai's fiery mount I flew;
But justice cried, with frowning face:
"This mountain is no Hiding Place."

Ere long a heavenly voice I heard,
And Mercy's angel soon appeared;
He led me at a placid pace,
To Jesus as a Hiding Place.

28

On Him almighty vengeance fell
Which must have sunk a world to Hell.
He bore it for a sinful race,
And thus became their Hiding Place.

Should sevenfold storms of thunder roll,
And shake this globe from pole to pole,
No thunderbolt shall daunt my face,
For Jesus is my Hiding Place.

A few more rolling suns at most,
Shall land me on fair Canaan's coast,
When I shall sing the song of grace,
And see my glorious Hiding Place.

MY GUEST

The day is fixed that there shall come to me
   A strange, mysterious guest;
The time I do not know—he keeps the date—
So all I have to do is work and wait,
   And keep me at my best,
And do my common duties patiently.

I've often wondered if that day would break
   Brighter than other days,
That I might know, or wrapped in some strange
   gloom.
And if he'd find me waiting in my room,
   Or busy with life's ways;
With weary hands and closing eyes that ached.

For many years I've know that he would come,
   And so I've watched for him,
And sometimes even said, "He will come soon,"
Yet mornings pass, followed by afternoon,
   With twilight dusk and dim,
And silent night-times, when the world is dumb,

But he will come, and find me here or there,
   It does not matter where,
For when he comes I know that he will take
In his these very hands of mine that ache
   (They will be idle then)
Just folded, may be, with a silent prayer.

Yes, he whom I expect has been called Death,
　　And once he is my guest,
Nothing disturbs of what has been or is;
I'll leave the world's loud company for his,
　　As that which seemeth best—
And none may hear the tender words he saith.

As we pass out, my royal guest and I,
　　As noiseless as he came,
For naught will do but I must go with him,
And leave the house I've lived in closed and dim,
I've known I should not need it by and by!

And so I sleep and wake, I toil and rest,
　　Knowing when he shall come
My Elder Brother will have sent for me,
Bidding him say that they especially
　　Have need of me at home;
And so I shall go gladly with my guest.

31

THERE IS NO DEATH

There is no death! The stars go down
    To rise upon some fairer shore;
And bright in Heaven's jewelled crown
    They shine forevermore.

There is no death! The dust we tread
    Shall change beneath the summer showers,
To golden grain or mellowed fruit,
    Or rainbow-tinted flowers.

The granite rocks disorganize,
    And feed the hungry moss they bear;
The forest leaves drink daily life,
    From out the viewless air.

There is no death! The leaves may fall,
    And flowers may fade and pass away;
They only wait through wintry hours,
    The coming of the May.

There is no death! An angel form
    Walks o'er the earth with silent tread;
He bears our best loved things away;
    And we then call them "dead."

He leaves our hearts all desolate,
    He plucks our fairest, sweetest flowers;
Transplanted into bliss, they now
    Adorn immortal bowers.

The bird-like voice, whose joyous tones,
　　Made glad these scenes of sin and strife,
Sings now an everlasting song,
　　Around the tree of life.

Where'er He sees a smile too bright,
　　Or heart too pure for taint and vice,
He bears it to that world of light,
　　To dwell in Paradise.

Born unto that undying life,
　　They leave us but to come again;
With joy we welcome them the same—
　　Except their sin and pain.

And ever near us, though unseen,
　　The dear immortal spirits tread;
For all the boundless universe
　　Is life—there are no dead.

WE MEET AT ONE GATE

We meet at one gate
When all's over. The ways they are many and wide,
And seldom are two ways the same. Side by side
May we stand at the same little door when all's
    done.

The ways they are many, the end it is one.
He that knocketh shall enter; who asks shall obtain;
And who seeketh, he findeth.

    *   *   *   *   *   *

No stream from its source
Flows seaward, how lonely so ever its course,
But what some land is gladdened. No star ever rose
And set without influence somewhere. Who knows
What earth needs from earth's lowest creature? No
    life
Can be pure in its purpose and strong in its strife
And all life not be purer and stronger thereby.
The spirits of just men made perfect on high,
The army of martyrs who stand by the Throne
And gaze into the face that makes glorious their
    own,
Know this, surely at last. Honest love, honest
sorrow,
Honest work for the day, honest hope for the
morrow,
Are these worth nothing more than the hand they
    make weary.

The heart they have saddened, the life they leave
    dreary?
Hush! the sevenfold heavens to the voice of the
    spirit
Echo: "He that o'ercometh shall all things inherit."

Owen Meredith

JUST BE GLAD

Oh! heart of mine, we shouldn't worry so!
What we have missed of calm, we couldn't have,
    you know!
    What we have met of stormy pain,
    And of sorrow's driving rain,
    We can better meet again,
        If they blow.

We have erred in that dark hour, we have known;
When the tears fell with the showers, all alone,
    Were not shine and shadow blent
    As the gracious Master meant?
    Let us temper our content
        With His own.

For we know not every morrow can be sad;
So, forgetting all the sorrow we have had,
    Let us fold away our fears
    And put by our foolish tears,
    And through all the coming years,
        Just be glad.

James Whitcomb Riley

THE LAST GATE

"The tomb is but the gateway to an eternity of opportunity."

THERE ARE LOYAL HEARTS

There are loyal hearts, there are spirits brave,
  There are souls that are pure and true;
Then give to the world the best you have,
  And the best shall come back to you.

Give love, and love to your heart will flow,
  A strength in your utmost need;
Have faith, and a score of hearts will show
  Their faith in your word and deed.

For life is the mirror of king and slave,
  'Tis just what you are and do;
Then give to the world the best you have,
  And the best will come back to you.

UPON THE VALLEY'S LAP

Upon the valley's lap
  The dewy morning throws
A thousand pearly drops
  To wake a single rose.

So, often in the course
  Of life's few fleeting years,
A single pleasure costs
  The soul a thousand tears.

"UNTIL THE DAYBREAK"

A human soul went forth into the night,
  Shutting behind it Death's mysterious door,
And shaking off, with strange, resistless might
    The dust that once it wore.
So swift its flight, so suddenly it sped—
  As when by skillful hand a bow is bent
The arrow flies—those watching round the bed
    Marked not the way it went.

Heavy with grief, their aching, tear-dimmed eyes
  Saw but the shadow fall, and knew not when,
Or in what fair or unfamiliar guise,
    It left the world of men.
It broke from sickness, that with iron bands
  Had bound it fast for many a grievous day;
And love itself with its restraining hands
    Might not its course delay.

Space could not hold it back with fettering bars,
  Time lost its power, and ceased at last to be;
It swept beyond the boundary of the stars,
    And touched Eternity.
Out from the house of mourning faintly lit,
  It passed upon its journey all alone;
So far not even thought could follow it
    Into those realms unknown.

Through the clear silence of the moonless dark,
  Leaving no footprint of the road it trod,
Straight as an arrow cleaving to its mark,
    The soul went home to God.
"Alas!" they cried, "he never saw the morn,
  But fell asleep outwearied with the strife"—
Nay, rather, he arose and met the dawn
    Of Everlasting Life.

SOMETIME

"What I do thou knowest not now, but thou shalt
know hereafter."

Sometime, when all life's lessons have been learned,
    And sun and stars forevermore have set,
The things which our weak judgment here have
    spurned,
The things o'er which we grieved with lashes wet,
Will flash before us, out of life's dark night,
    As stars shine more in deeper tints of blue,
And we shall see how all God's plans were right,
    And how what seemed reproof was love most
    true.

And we shall see how, while we frown and sigh,
    God's plans go on as best for you and me;
How, when we called, He heeded not our cry,
    Because His wisdom to the end could see.
And even as prudent parents disallow
    Too much of sweet to craving babyhood,
So God, perhaps, is keeping from us now
    Life's sweetest things, because it seemeth good.

And if, sometimes commingled with life's wine,
    We find the wormwood and rebel and shrink,
Be sure a wiser hand than yours or mine
    Pours out this potion for our lips to drink.

And if some friend we love is lying low,
   Where human kisses cannot reach his face,
Oh, do not blame the loving Father so!
   But wear your sorrow with obedient grace.

And you shall shortly know that lengthened breath
   Is not the sweetest gift God sends His friend,
And that sometimes the sable pall of death
   Conceals the fairest boon His love can send.
If we could push ajar the gates of life
   And stand within and all God's workings see,
We could interpret all this doubt and strife,
   And for each mystery could find a key.

But not today. Then be content, poor heart!
   God's plans, like lilies, pure and white unfold.
We must not tear the close-shut leaves apart;
   Time will reveal the hidden cups of gold,
And if through patient toil we reach the land,
   Where weary feet, with sandals loosed, may rest,
Then shall we know and clearly understand—
   I think that we shall say, "God knew the best."

THE CREATOR IN CREATION

I am the mote in the sunbeam, and I am the burning
    sun;
"Rest here!" I whisper the atom; I call to the orb,
    "Roll on!"
I am the blush of morning, and I am the evening
    breeze,
I am the leaf's low murmur, the swell of the terrible
    seas.
I am the net, the fowler, the bird and its frightened
    cry,
The mirror, the form reflected, the sound and its
    echo, I;
The lover's passionate pleading, the maiden's
    whispered fear,
The warrior, the blade that smites him, his mother's
    heartwrung tear.
I am intoxication, grapes, wine-press, and must,
    and wine,
The guest, the host, the tavern, the goblet of crystal
    fine;
I am the breath of the flute, and I am the mind
    of man,
Gold's glitter, the light of the diamond, the sea
    pearl's lustre wan;
The rose, her poet nightingale, the songs from his
    throat that rise,
Flint sparks, the flame, the taper, the moth that
about it flies.
I am both Good and Evil; the deed, and deed's
    intent,

Temptation, victim, sinner, crime, pardon and
   punishment;
I am what was, is, will be; creation's ascent and
   fall;
The link, the chain of existence; beginning and
   end of All!

THE CHOIR INVISIBLE

O may I join the choir invisible
Of those immortal dead who live again
In minds made better by their presence; live
In pulses stirred to generosity,
In deeds of daring rectitude, in scorn
For miserable aims that end with self,
In thoughts sublime that pierce the night like stars,
And with their mild persistence urge man's search
To vaster issues.
             So to live is Heaven;
To make undying music in the world,
Breathing as beauteous order that controls
With growing sway the growing life of man.
So we inherit that sweet purity
For which we struggled, failed and agonized
With widening retrospect that bred despair.
Rebellious flesh that would not be subdued,
A vicious parent shaming still its child,
Poor anxious penitence is quick dissolved;
Its discords, quenched by meeting harmonies,
Die in the large and charitable air.
And all our rarer, better, truer self,
That sobbed religiously in yearning song,
That watched to ease the burden of the world,
Laboriously tracing what must be,
And what may yet be better—saw within
A worthier image for the sanctuary,
And shaped it forth before the multitude
Divinely human, raising worship so

To higher reverence more mixed with love—
That better self shall live till human Time
Shall fold its eyelids, and the human sky
Be gathered like a scroll within the tomb
Unread forever.

   This is life to come,
Which martyred men have made more glorious
For us who strive to follow. May I reach
That purest heaven, be to other souls
The cup of strength in some great agony,
Enkindle generous ardor, feed pure love,
Beget the smiles that have no cruelty—
Be the sweet presence of a good diffused,
And in diffusion ever more intense.
So shall I join the choir invisible
Whose music is the gladness of the world.

George Eliot

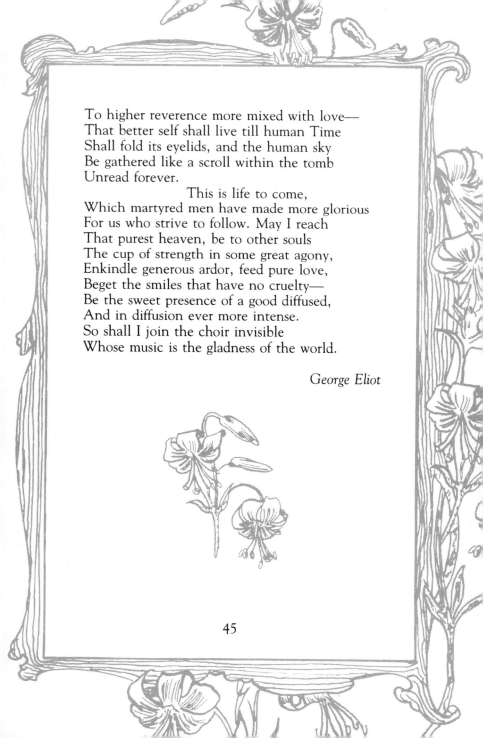

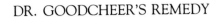

DR. GOODCHEER'S REMEDY

Feel all out of kilter, do you?
    Nothing goes to suit you quite?
Skies seem sort of dark and clouded,
    Though the day is fair and bright?
Eyes affected, fail to notice
    Beauty spread on every hand?
Hearing so impaired you're missing
    Songs of promise, sweet and grand?

No! your case is not uncommon—
    'Tis a popular distress;
Though 'tis not at all contagious,
    Thousands have it more or less.
But it yields to simple treatment,
    And is easy quite to cure;
If you follow my directions,
    Quickly recovery is sure.

Take a bit of cheerful thinking,
    Add a portion of content,
And with both let glad endeavor,
    Mixed with earnestness, be blent;
These, with care and skill compounded,
    Will produce a magic oil
That is bound to cure, if taken
    With a lot of honest toil.

If your heart is dull and heavy;
　　If your hope is pale with doubt;
Try this wondrous Oil of Promise,
　　For 'twill drive the evil out.
Who will mix it? Not the druggist
　　From the bottles on his shelf;
The ingredients required
You must find within yourself.

RECESSIONAL

God of our fathers, known of old—
    Lord of our far-flung battle-line—
Beneath whose awful hand we hold
    Dominion over palm and pine—
Lord God of Hosts, be with us yet,
Lest we forget—lest we forget!

The tumult and the shouting dies—
    The captains and the kings depart—
Still stands Thine ancient Sacrifice,
    An humble and a contrite heart.
Lord God of Hosts, be with us yet,
Lest we forget—lest we forget!

Far-called our navies melt away—
    On dune and headline sinks the fire—
Lo, all our pomp of yesterday
    Is one with Nineveh and Tyre!
Judge of the Nations, spare us yet,
Lest we forget—lest we forget!

If, drunk with sight of power, we loose
    Wild tongues that have not Thee in awe—
Such boasting as the Gentiles use
    Or lesser breeds without the Law—
Lord God of Hosts, be with us yet,
Lest we forget—lest we forget!

For heathen heart that puts her trust
  In reeking tube and iron shard—
All valiant dust that builds on dust,
  And guarding calls not Thee to guard—
For frantic boast and foolish word,
Thy Mercy on Thy People, Lord!

Amen.

Rudyard Kipling

NEARER, MY GOD, TO THEE

Nearer, my God, to Thee,
 Nearer to Thee!
E'en though it be a cross
 That raiseth me;
Still all my song shall be,
Nearer, my God, to Thee,
 Nearer to Thee!

Though like the wanderer,
 The sun gone down,
Darkness be over me,
 My rest a stone;
Yet in my dreams I'd be
Nearer, my God, to Thee,
 Nearer to Thee!

There let the way appear,
 Steps unto heaven;
All that Thou sendest me
 In mercy given;
Angels to beckon me
Nearer, my God, to Thee,
 Nearer to Thee!

Then, with my waking thoughts
 Bright with Thy praise,
Out of my stony griefs,
 Bethel I'll raise
So by my woes to be

Nearer, my God, to Thee,
  Nearer to Thee!

Or if, on joyful wing,
  Cleaving the sky,
Sun, moon and stars forgot,
  Upward I fly;
Still all my song shall be,
Nearer, my God, to Thee,
  Nearer to Thee!

HOW DID YOU DIE?

Did you tackle the trouble that came your way
    With a resolute heart and cheerful?
Or hide your face from the light of day
    With a craven soul and fearful?
Oh, a trouble's a ton, or a trouble's an ounce,
    Or a trouble is what you make it,
And it isn't the fact that you're hurt that counts,
    But only how did you take it?

You are beaten to earth? Well, well, what's that?
    Come up with a smiling face.
It's nothing against you to fall down flat,
    But to lie there—that's disgrace.
The harder you're thrown, why, the higher you
    bounce;
    Be proud of your blackened eye!
It isn't the fact that you're licked that counts;
    It's how did you fight—and why?

And though you be done to the death, what then?
    If you battled the best you could,
If you played your part in the world of men,
    Why, the Critic will call it good.
Death comes with a crawl, or comes with a pounce,
    And whether he's slow or spry,
It isn't the fact that you're dead that counts,
    But only how did you die?

WE SEE WITH OUR VISION IMPERFECT

We see with our vision imperfect,
    Such causes of dread or fear,
Some that are far in the distance,
    And some that may never be near;
When if we would trust in His wisdom,
    Whose purpose we cannot see,
We would find, whatever our trial,
    As our day, our strength shall be.

ON THE TWENTY-THIRD PSALM

In "pastures green"? Not always; sometimes He
Who knoweth best, in kindness leadeth me
In weary ways, where heavy shadows be.

And by "still waters"? No, not always so;
Oft-times the heavy tempests round me blow.
And o'er my soul the waves and billows go.

But when the storms beat loudest, and I cry
Aloud for help, the Master standeth by,
And whispers to my soul, "Lo, it is I!"

So, where He leads me, I can safely go.
And in the blest hereafter I shall know
Why, in His wisdom, He had led me so.

JESUS, LOVER OF MY SOUL

Jesus, Lover of my soul,
 Let me to Thy bosom fly,
While the nearer waters roll,
 While the tempest still is high;
Hide me, O my Saviour, hide
 Till the storm of life is past;
Safe into the haven guide,
 O receive my soul at last.

Other refuge have I none;
 Hangs my helpless soul on Thee;
Leave, ah! leave me not alone,
 Still support and comfort me.
All my trust on Thee is stayed,
 All my help from Thee I bring;
Cover my defenceless head
 With the shadow of Thy wing.

Wilt Thou not regard my call?
 Wilt Thou not accept my prayer?
Lo, I sink, I faint, I fall!
 Lo, on Thee I cast my care;
Reach me out Thy gracious hand!
 While I of Thy strength receive,
Hoping against hope I stand,
 Dying, and behold I live!

Thou, O Christ, art all I want;
  More than all in Thee I find;
Raise the fallen, cheer the faint,
  Heal the sick and lead the blind.
Just and holy is Thy name;
  I am all unrighteousness;
False and full of sin I am,
  Thou art full of truth and grace.

Plenteous grace with Thee is found,
  Grace to cover all my sin;
Let the healing streams abound,
  Make and keep me pure within.
Thou of life the Fountain art,
  Freely let me take of Thee;
Spring Thou up within my heart,
  Rise to all eternity.

Charles Wesley

A PSALM OF LIFE

Tell me not in mournful numbers,
  "Life is but an empty dream!"
For the soul is dead that slumbers,
  And things are not what they seem.

Life is real! Life is earnest!
  And the grave is not its goal;
"Dust thou art, to dust returnest,"
  Was not spoken of the soul.

Not enjoyment and not sorrow,
  Is our destined end or way;
But to act, that each tomorrow
  Find us farther than today.

Art is long, and time is fleeting,
  And our hearts, though stout and brave,
Still, like muffled drums are beating
  Funeral marches to the grave.

In the world's broad field of battle,
  In the bivouac of life,
Be not like dumb, driven cattle!
  Be a hero in the strife!

Trust no future, howe'er pleasant!
  Let the dead past bury its dead!
Act, act in the living present!
  Heart within and God o'erhead!

Lives of great men all remind us
  We can make our lives sublime,
And, departing, leave behind us
  Footprints on the sands of time.

Footprints, that perhaps another,
  Sailing o'er life's solemn main,
A forlorn and shipwrecked brother,
  Seeing, shall take heart again.

Let us, then, be up and doing,
  With a heart for any fate;
Still achieving, still pursuing,
  Learn to labor and to wait.

Henry W. Longfellow

BEREAVED

Let me come in where you sit weeping—aye
Let me, who have not any child to die,
Weep with you for the little one whose love
I have known nothing of.

The little arms that slowly, slowly loosed
Their pressure round your neck; the hands you used
To kiss—such arms, such hands I never knew,
May I not weep with you?

Fain would I be of service—say something,
Between the tears, that would be comforting—
But ah! so sadder than yourself am I
Who have no child to die!

James Whitcomb Riley

WHO NE'ER HAS SUFFERED

Who ne'er has suffered, he has lived but half.
  Who never failed, he never strove or sought.
Who never wept is stranger to a laugh.
  And he who never doubted never thought.